The Lovely Disciplines
Martyn Crucefix

SEREN

Seren is the book imprint of
Poetry Wales Press Ltd.
57 Nolton Street, Bridgend, Wales, CF31 3AE
www.serenbooks.com
facebook.com/SerenBooks
twitter@SerenBooks

The right of Martyn Crucefix to be identified as
the author of this work has been asserted in accordance
with the Copyright, Designs and Patents Act, 1988.

© Martyn Crucefix, 2017

ISBN: 978-1-78172-389-0
ebook: 978-1-78172-390-6
Kindle: 978-1-78172-391-3

A CIP record for this title is available from the British Library.

The publisher acknowledges the financial assistance of the Welsh Books Council.

Cover Artwork: Tom Crucefix (Year 6)

Printed by Airdrie Print Services Ltd.

Author Website: www.martyncrucefix.com

Contents

I Scree We Ride

II The Lovely Disciplines

III Boy-racer

I
Scree We Ride

Aubade

from a song

We reverse the type
you relinquish me
the man turns back
to the warmth of pillows

to the shrinking hearth
of his lover's gone heat
the front door below
swings open and shut

I listen to your shoes
where they crack stones
along the front path
the car lock shot back

and vividly I see
how you approach
right hand outstretched
the engine's note

whines and dwindles
unpicking our warmth
where you've woken
to worlds of fact

of metal and time
where friction wears
where rust never sleeps
where three follows two

where our lips let slip
where cursors blink
into day's brute dawn
as with this one's alarm

this brash disarray
of moments to come
bringing the taste of coin
and keys to my tongue

The little dances

I glimpse a strange truck
in the nearside lane
with a soiled ribbed hose
wound on a two-metre reel
like a toy fire engine—
and up close to the cab
balanced and symmetrical
a pair of translucent
sepia-coloured tanks
I can't imagine what for
but swirling with what seems
no more than water
as the truck crawls
on the Great Cambridge Road
the sun's rays crack
and split and sashay
in each tank as the truck
stops and starts the little dance
between brake and pedal
each vehicle performs
and as I draw alongside
the liquid shows that frisk
of light now more fluently
full of refracting bows
and slabs and S-shapes
like glittering lemon bars
anaemic and urinous
and rather than the road
I see a man who was dying
who'd lost his sight
who I sat with sometimes
maybe twenty years ago
and then imagined
how I might be his eyes
having words to convey
what he would never see
though my mouth stayed
shut I kept my eyes open

R–O–M–J–X

She asks *is it better with or better without*
her glass in his eyes like sweets in his mouth

the woman moving in a dim-lit room
barely visible yet she insists on breathing

through the long defence of his privacy
how he loves it when she blows air in his eye

happy when he's asked to concentrate
on the balloon she conjures on a glass screen

its vivid reds above the white stripe of road
set him dreaming of imagined Americas

murmuring in pastel shades now she crowds
voices pleasure whether he's right or wrong

wants him to spell out her strange words
though this morning she does not ask him

to number the white streak of falling stars
to his disappointment has no reason

to gentle his head into the rubber clamps
though he submits to the dazzling of her lamp

is it the red she asks *is it the red or the green*
O how he loves her vocabulary of absolutes

On Stukeley Street

At the corner in passing find a pile of rags
that stinks of no one's urine

but his own... this ragged man and what
impulse is this to stop and stare

as he scans the map spread before him
as he turns to the hundred and fifth degree

to the Northwest Territories—
to them he raises his shrivelled arms

as if to lift and tense an unseen bow
to them he pulls back and still further back

till with a delicate touch
on his blackened earlobe suddenly lets go

to Yellowknife to Inuvik
to the Great Bear and the Great Slave

to the Mackenzie river to what his outward eye
has never seen to what he'd bring

crashing down into this dusty street
all the cold the blue the unconditional flood

Scree we ride

You say we have had too much of rock
have placed our feet on it though often
disguised as moss and soil as grass
or dust but rock it is that holds us up
and rock it is that has raised itself
to these inclines eroded to leave naked
these jags and shards that trip us up
and rock it is we scuff as gravel
rock that we clamber up like steps
rock as scree we ride only half in control
till we have had enough of rock
with its little abstracts of lemon lichen
its runnings-off in rust red in streams
its slate-eye dark beneath the gleaming tarn
and rock re-shaping every skyline
as much as these three inches square
where I intend to steady my foot
and rock grows glossy under a brief shower
warm to the touch in its hour of sun
rock hollowed by the work of hands
in search of tin or iron or gold
until rock is wealth for a brief time
till it can yield up nothing more
and really rock is the one in the many
if I pick a pebble I feel its weight
I carry it in my pocket as reminder
of what flows in veins props my bones
the grumbling ache in my right hip
it runs at night under my dreams
the blackbird ticking in a tree soon to leaf
it is the leaf it is the slate roof beyond
it is the blue smoke
slouching from red pots above me
the slope of the distant fell-side's blue
its sparse covering of pine and gorse
its carpets of moss and soil and grass
its dust compacted where I recover
each fumbled foothold it's where I'll rest
my bones how can we have too much of rock

Mitigation

Our French-speaking German student guide
moves tall and thin through the Grottes de Sare

making a couple of apologetic asides—
the first to say *sorry but by regulation*

it must be that I must speak only in French—
with the second he makes a longer breach

turning from his spiel on stalactites
that we take for granted must be absolutes

falling by definition to the vertical
he explains they bend sometimes if the breeze

predominant through the cavern system
loosens the grip that gravity takes

on every droplet depositing its speck
of calcium carbonate at the sensitive tip

under such conditions those hanging forms
incline to strangely beautiful curves

not levitation he smiles *more mitigation*
though by now I'm less convinced

of his command of the English language
of what he can or cannot have possibly said

As we live

In this second-hand copy of Mary Oliver's *Swan*
I discover a year-old ATM receipt

and though I've never banked with NatWest
it tells me there is a balance of

thirty-six thousand three hundred and forty-five
the slip of paper suggests I turn it over

and beside the key to its cryptic codings
I find scrawled *crisps frankfurters*

cherries prawnies soup—
after the hole in the wall she jotted this list

perhaps over coffee a quiet reading of *Swan*
though the spine of the book is barely creased

so perhaps she did not take to its leaves
its foxes bears birds its nod to Emerson—

we only believe as deep as we live—but drifted
to devise a meal of frankfurters and cherries

to ponder her use of the diminutive
her childhood self weirdly naked in the slip

of the pen in *prawnies*—for that moment
visible above the well-defended parapets

of wife and mother and salaried worker
a little match-flicker of identification

the ripple and pulse of dumb invertebrate life
that may or may not have been rapidly snuffed

These things I remember

after Jesse Berridge

That afternoon on the beach at Kilve
we had ascertained
there was no weather-cock on the church
and we were resting in peace
almost in silence when he turned
and told me to listen
to the little melodious twittering
of a tiny bird that swooped and dipped
between where we sat and the roiling ocean—
a meadow pipit he said
the moment was unforgettable then
as he so often made such things
calling attention to this or that aspect
of what I call his vision
as one morning he cut a walking-stick
from the woods then carved
until it had a character of its own
or the knife I've owned almost sixty years
its bone handle chafed
and worn by my touch
until the white has begun to show through
for him held a peculiar fascination
till obscurely I began to feel
it possessed of a soul
that nothing but his observation of it
had created and I remember my children
always delighted in his occasional visit

Nightlights

Once inside she asks to light a candle
and though they're meant for prayer
I whisper there's no problem
just as long as she can make a wish
as she might come March
for her seventh birthday

if with a bit more reverence—
though that's not exactly what I say—
but we can't find a spill to bring the flame
and they're not real candles anyway
in her little daunted hands
she finds the tiny nightlights

too fiddly to kindle
one from another so I take the lead
without thinking ease her gently aside
steadying a nightlight in each hand
this one held up dark and unlit
this one already brightly trembling

as if I've a firm grip at last
on the great dualities she begins to divine
yet edging them closer
the flame shrugs and promptly gutters
starved of air of course
and so we laugh but then hush

with the shock of having snuffed out
someone else's fervent prayer
with our attempt to light our own
and not only because hers must be
the more light-hearted one—
we each feel everything here has weight

In 'Any Amount of Books'

Here on the Charing Cross Road
I pick out a biography
of Hopkins from the cheap bins outside
then tinkling the bell

of the sticking door into the dark
I address myself to the counter—
you know it of course
with its bar room flip-up lowered today

barring my progress
into the stockroom's wild trove of books
its boxes of second-hand books
its babels of toppling

abandoned books its slews of books
assembling like timid creatures
as my eyes adjust to the gloom
finally to conjure the shape

of a bent man stooping like a heron
over one dusty carton
and he seems to be speaking to me
because the shop is empty

on this wet Wednesday afternoon
there's no one else to be seen
so he's addressing me when he says
I've the Catholic Church

I've another complete history
of the Western Church but yes I do
have it here would you like
to take it now the Catholic Church

Reading Hass on Milosz

... if he meant "Oh!" or "O!"

I'm first to confess it
Oh! is longer drawn already
beginning the button-down
of understanding
that well-I-never
with its freighting
of verb tense and identity
whereas O! is more sudden
more urgent surely
of the moment rapt
when we are prised open
by desire as I am here
in Oddbins where I choose
this bottle of red
though not for myself
but my daughter's cello teacher
since she's to be replaced
by one more challenging
or at least he comes trailing
an Eastern European name
like Vaclav or Pavel
or simply Pal—
so while I stand here
handing the dark bottle
across to the assistant
in her maroon vest
only now am I hearing
the loose-limbed clatter
of jazz on the speakers
though it's been there all along
A Night in Tunisia
or *Ornithology*
as she stares at me with
no more than the desire
to serve yet sees my eyes
widen and the tiny up-tilt

of my chin and you'd
forgive her for thinking
that she was the focus
of my arousing when really
she's just a fragment
I say equal to these others
she's no more if no less
a part of the O! I am

Valsaintes

On two or three occasions every day
four donkeys in the field below the house

set up such a braying for all to hear
their broadcasting of guttural chest noise

alternating on the in-breath
with such a screech in the throat

and this is the noise of the twisted bolt
to the abandoned cellar beneath the house

its long thin penis-length
of rusted orange-brown worked up and down

in its cradle to reach a squalling pitch
till it can be loosened and drawn

and these are the sounds I hear at dawn
of ancient Yves about the wood-pile

his fleshy shoulders pumping the saw
remote in the silence of a hard-pressed man

the throaty growl of metal on the back stroke
more of a squeal each time he leans in

The renovation near Sansepolcro

I choose the terrace from which to read everything
where it swivels towards me

with the fury of a blow-torch
the unevenness of a candle till I lose myself

in the caves of blue shadow beneath the fig tree
the swallow's cross-stitch down the valley

the pale swimmer's supine turning to heave
the billow of her watery echo

up and down the pool beneath the wires hanging
slack from the green parade

of telegraph poles—the cold calls locked inside
the surfing of voices in air-conditioned cells

oblivious to the baying of this heat—
until I hear her feet as she brushes hot stones

along the path until I listen to the noise
one leaf makes or the whisper

of ants exploring the hairy terrain of my feet
or the picture postcard she bought

this morning I use for a bookmark—
the hyperopthalmic gaze

of Piero's risen Christ standing like a swimmer
in his off-the-shoulder pink shift

like a builder with one foot planted firm and flat
on the tomb he rises like spring-water

like a wintry candle his firm grip
on the flagged staff where to one side of him

stand winter trees to the other worlds of leaf

After Bonnefoy

Love—let's find ourselves at such
a height as if light spilled
from the hour's vessel the mingling cries
a bright stream where nothing stays

but abundance itself so designated
let's unearth ourselves and seize
on the bed of morning the bed of evening
handfuls of sheer pure presence

wherever time gouges its furrows
where the precise waters vanish into air
let's bring ourselves one to another

as if each was at last all creatures
and all things all empty ways
all stones all metals and all streams

Nocturne

in black and yellow

With this your coming to me in the dark
we are the dimming fragments
each frantic for those minutes
each the burning fragments too
of this our tiny domestic festival
in the black-out of a slope-beamed room
its walls an impenetrable metre thick
pierced by windows we open each night
to welcome the dark

to fill it with every shred of ourselves
though subject still
to the pull of gravity
as the moments promenade about us
when nothing resembles its daytime order
re-composing ourselves
in our fullest forms our most spindly forms
we re-configure the poet's kelson

our hold-fast no matter which of us
sprawls prone no matter which
lies supine as for an age it seems to pass
even for the worms below
where they are drawn to the forest of grass
to the same glistening of moisture
the window-gleam of night's angled moon
until the greater light
touches the leaves begins to speak

of itself as irrepressible dawn
and with its breaking of yolk-yellow
across the horizon we too—my darling—
we too must have succumbed
to this ordinary speech that must prove
good enough to find our way
to rise to work to hunger alone
so long as it mouths us eagerly back again

II
The Lovely Disciplines

Skype

Over the patchwork levels of eastern England
that familiar image
of a banking Spitfire beyond their shoulders
between them it roars
as the war bound them sixty years together
loving to talk though struggling still
to unmute to get the camera going
yet it's better this way
since he sees who's talking more easily
he can be more involved
though sometimes the laptop screen
is angled so I catch only the crowns
of grey heads then a giant hand
reaches forward to re-adjust
re-appears holding *The Wiltshire Times*
its crashes and floods and marriages
and something else too blurred
even if the connection holds
but if it wavers faces split to stained glass
or cubist fragments or fairground mirrors
still talking blithely asking me still
if I can see these crocuses
the lawn in sunshine their bird table
where sparrows in pairs come for food and drink

Rebuilding Tellisford weir

turn aside to see Tellisford – Edward Thomas

He refuses shade in midday heat
the old man walking
in his honey-brimmed hat
along the drained weir-shelf

that looks today like stacked loaves
its pallid smooth ranks
of Victorian stones
mapping precisely the Domesday line

where he patrols to and fro
proudly surveying the place he owns
this stretch of England
his plan to restore the workings

of the old watermill
to feed the Grid—and it is for this
he has ordered tons of sludge
to be dredged above the drop

and dozens of loosened stones
to be replaced to give
the mill-race its full head
and today he walks the slippery length

of the dammed weir-shelf
hallooing picnickers
who pull corks from fizzy wines
he cries *what marvellous weather*

then falls to conversation with a couple
who are celebrating sixty years
in their self-built house
with their three good boys

raised and schooled to distant homes
though today they recline
on trashy garden chairs
on this riverbank as if to watch

the old man in an antique yellow hat
who walks noting progress
on the weir and how could they know
he's something on his mind

for the next hundred years
how could they know more and more
these days he struggles to endure
the roaring of the fish-shoot

with its silted water
and these stilted conversations
with such ordinary people
their Diet Coke and egg mayonnaise

their crisps for the grandchildren
their Sunday newspapers
let blow and tumble across the meadow
reminding him of himself

how his mind often strays
up the ditch-line to the old drovers' road
where for fifty years
their cars have pinked and purred

especially at night as they mount
slowly the gravel verge—
O so many love-cars for so many years
drawn to his father's land

each in pursuit of what the river gives
of moonlight and chance
of the ticking of an engine
as it cools of blonde hair spilling

across dark seats in disarray
he knows the windows rolled to the dusk
the sickly smell of water
the murmur within and talk

when it's over though he knows well
it is never really over—
and it's because of this
he will not turn them away

although they holler and soil and litter
still he'd grant them every wish
it's for this his feet edge now across
the weir-shelf this afternoon

for this he takes his uneasy stand
hands thrust in his pockets
their cars pulling in to the dark hiss
of white gravel everywhere loosening

Words and things

Past ninety and still no books to read
your knuckles rap the laid table

gestures beside a stumble of words
so much aware of their inadequacy

it hurts us both in different ways
since a man without language is no man

finding too late this absence of words
builds a prison you're no longer able

to dominate objects as once you did
the world turns in your loosening grip

The toll cottage

Dad and I are driving out of Trowbridge
he's at the wheel having come up Timbrell Street
along Islington with nothing amiss
but as we turn to take the next incline
up beyond the thatched toll cottage
I glance to my right past his concentrating head
and to my surprise see green space
where there should be nothing but suburban brick
a green valley slipping down and away
towards a distinct hill
punctuated by dark trees
and straight runs of hedges or perhaps
at this distance are they impossible vines
and my sole thought is to rationalise—
my home-town landscape changed again
but already we're climbing past the toll
at the top of the incline to hit the brow of the hill
with that lightening that little hoopla stir
in our bellies as the mass
of our bodies continues to rise
while the weight of the car hugs the earth
and we lift in consequence from our seats
only to be set down—now we rumble
along a grassy ridge and the road has vanished
to open sky though there are signs still
declaring Coventry or Daventry
it's impossible to make them out and Dad
at the wheel has not missed a beat
though it's fifteen years since he was street-legal
and in alarm I turn saying *this is bad*
look this is really bad but he has dealt
more easily with our translation than his son

Into northern light

Roaring unknown north how to make a mark
what bites him what wakes him in the dark

as today passing car after powerful car
he glimpses the campus where he first met her

waiting beside the lift her lips and lank hair
her welcoming smile for each gauche Fresher

he was one of those who came and went
joking how she walked from her hips her cunt

thrust forward in open invitation
though she chose who she might bestow it on

he was not one and where is she now
twenty-five years older and nowhere he'd know

perhaps driving her kids to Freshers' Week
leaving her old man content with his work

O this northern light spills across the day
like butter in the grass how it slips away

like buttons on her blouse grazing sheep stand
while he guns through unnoticed as the wind

accelerating north and how to make a mark
still what wakes him in the road-killing dark

A long barrow in Wiltshire

From across the ridgeline
far off military firing
the crack of a sheet
of a heavy door slamming

sounds from the house
you've just driven from
where Mum and Dad
live ever more confined

you've parked the car
but in the cloven entrance
a buzz and agitation
as if to dissuade

till the bee's repelled
by damp and darkness
permitting you to pass
to shadow-pods of spaces

long since exposed to air
now sky-lit from above
not a soul comes near
you sense the need

to empty yourself
across the ground outside
a glittering yellow stream
as if to persuade

a thousand bowing leaves
of grass to assent
to the black soil where
your borrowings fade

you see how others
prefer the proximal oak
hung with knotted ribbons
stones tied with string

two ears of barley
a handkerchief offering
sweet wrappers here
a hospital wristband

The house of your parents as a waterfall

On the familiar road
towards childhood home
you walk and you know your way to the tears

that are most to be found
on the rainbow brink
where you find the way things are now

cannot be the way that things were then
you tread the pavement
beside the old road

though cars pass much less frequently now
you cross the tarmac
to the sunken ditch

awash in May-time with Queen Anne's Lace
and what you called 'snake's food'
in the sweet hedge—

beyond the baking fields of harvested bales
where children play
at castle battlements

at such serious play
on the look-out always for imagined foes
all the while blind

to how time slid across the stubble-fields
to be breathed in
and while it lay asleep

you walked out further
to the great waterfall
the original house where your parents live

where they move upstairs
across the landing
as if straining at something they heard

and she gazes then from the upper window
in such a silence
as there has never been—

on that first of days you find your way
to unlock the door
in this house for once

there is no one calling
no inquisition on the state of the roads
only this silence

breathed in years ago
you bring out now to examine what's said
by way of silence

with its speaking tongue
its grammars stirring while it remains
till the day it rises

it walks out it swims
it betrays itself as speech to be heard
to be handed down

to your own children
though to them it appears
such speech they think it really silence

so they breathe it in
since they too have a way to go
where they fear what they come to find

The lovely disciplines

See Ginny's son and Ginny's daughter-in-law
rest useless hands on the raised bed-rail

stare down to where Ginny writhes and squirms
her slender left arm reaching O so high

while her bare right calf lies crooked across
the cold retaining bar as lucky Jane all day

scuts with her bird-like legs folded under
to clear the turning wheels of her chair

while she roams the ward her working shoulders
pump and shove as if she'd tear herself

from the purple seat while Michaela's throat
goes sucking great holes in the hospital air

rubbing itself raw till she's like a bull-seal
honking on a distant shore she might once

have defended open-eyed though none here
believes Michaela will stir—no brighter hope

any more for Linda where she's settled still
in her pink dressing-gown beside her bed

neat as a serviette her eyes fixed on a man
from her V of hands while he stares at her

from his V of hands at the woman he moved
coterminous with for years who now prefers

distance and darkness and being dumb—
O no more those lovely disciplines

we reassure ourselves it's human to pursue
and no more those sweet acts of will

we briefly treasure or take for granted
consoling ourselves that we will be spared

the horror of long blue rooms like these
the slack and supine and all this twaddle

of decay and so persuade ourselves
that the truth need not be so bleak

as it seems for these who hold the floor today
who turn hardly more than a leaf turns

in being blown to the gutter those who seem
as nothing to themselves if more to others

who come with names they won't let go
murmuring Ginny Michaela darling Linda Jane

This brooch

after Boris Pasternak

As if window-shopping
crowds block the way
stretcher swung aboard
paramedics in place

street shadows carved
by the ambulance's beam
city thunders past
police and pavements dancing

as doors swing on faces
gawping the nurse's grip
on the saline bottle
loosening as she tips

to and fro—snowfall
filling gutters quickly
paperwork in triplicate
the roar of A and E

★

Pushed to a corridor
she snuffs iodine smells
in the air-conditioning
as the ward fills

flash of pale uniform
windows catch her eye
glimpse of garden
beneath the rag of sky

she comes to know
the import of their stare
gently nodding heads
odds stacked against her

supine beneath the glare
her gaze at the wall
the flaring of streetlamps
weirdly grateful

she watches blinds close
branches of a tree
leaves lost to the wind
bowing her goodbye

★

Things are as they are
her prayer to the wall
streets death lights night
the enveloping hospital

twisted handkerchief
tears soaked through
drowsy sedatives
blur my sight of you

yet sweet to feel light
on my bed to see
myself my life my living it
as gifts lent me

hands close by
in good time to replace
this brooch this handiwork
in death's jewel-case

Your dark-haired daughter

In New Year's cold
of yesterday's white dawn
I opened the boot
of your old blue car
to gifts your daughter
bought doctors and nurses

in confident anticipation
in those bright days
just before Christmas
of the hour approaching
when you'd no longer
depend on their attention

would emerge blinking
into New Year's dazzle
its expanse of blue
after the airless space
of filthy wards
leaning hard on the arm

of your grateful husband
your dark-haired daughter
who tonight is shaking
beside me in bed
tears raw as earth-tremors
each one too fierce

for what I have to offer
a poor return till we
each lie barely breathing
in dread of February
with its sheets of snow
transforming the nature

of cars on the street
these gifts of chocolate
sweetly perfumed soap
a bottle of flame-hot
brandy grown cold
with the hours and more

dense with the cold
left untouched still
in the boot of your car
its amber dead-weight
like Spring itself
sprawled stiff in its bed

La Gioconda gone

*'Gone' by Bryan Eccleshall is an oil painting of the
space left by the theft of the Mona Lisa in 1911*

What you see is what will
happen in the end—
the moment we speed away
that last time

from the edifice of ourselves
hand clasped to hand
and in flight from daylight
in hope of leaving

a serene figure above forgotten feet
and closer to a finish
then we're given to others
for their consideration

those no longer lost in a lovely face
who must encounter
the thing that is
rather than the thing becoming

till they're drawn to contemplate
the extent to which
we rise above the horizon
how far we appear

in part natural outcrop
in larger part to our own design
though so much depends
upon desire

attentive open tender firm—
here a bridge crosses the water
witness her shade
and how she moves

all the time appearing
not to move—the slug of clay
beneath faultless flesh
a shadow now quick almost nothing

a maze of paths in the poplar wood
of airy clouds
to cloak the setting sun
laid deep as marrow in the bone

till they think of art as life
as all she's ever felt
all she's ever thought and done
just what's given to everyone

Script

Cars at the roadside
covering their heads
with snow as with ash
and who dares move
must slither on the hills
must stand in the road

to shrug as if lost
all things grown pale
all things resisting
the need to connect
the blue lids of snow
and water's divorce

from its subtler self
in the absence of heat
the length of your lawn
where it falls untouched
unless by the foxes
by the feet of birds

that print the script
of your returning
I sit quietly in the car
feel space become
cooler by the minute
each step unsteady

then shock at seeing
what seems a thin dog
gazing at the road
it shakes and retreats
up a drifting alley
lets slip a glimpse

of twinkling snow-melt
on its low red brush
as it moves as it must
as you must have gone
a blur of small feet
across the blank lawn

Afterwards

As well be underwater
pale bungalow hunkers down
buried under drifts of snow
no way round

green lawns frost over
a few grass spears show
driveway swept and clear
nowhere to go

all ways closed and barred
no gate or window ready
double-fronted garage door
shut steady...

steady... ride this out
this art of giving way
no root no branch no air
no light of day

a trellis buried flat
the size and shape of a coffin
children losing voice
how to begin

as well be underwater
pale bungalow hunkers down
buried under drifts of snow
no way round

House sold

We tramp up the garden
over sodden slippy grass
to three birches that mark the boundary

and someone might see us
bring fork and spade
and a black bin liner to the foot of the trees

where we eye mossy cushions
gravitate to this
barely visible mound where you point and speak

someone might glimpse me
as I slice open the earth
complicated by roots but in this spot

the spade slides in well
as if re-opening a hole
and someone might watch you crouch and scrape

your fingers stained dark
as you rake out soil
and I thrust in the fork—someone sees us

both on our knees now
like archaeologists
lifting an object the size of a sweet jar

maroon in colour
punctured by my fork
you take it wrap it in the black bin liner

then stand and wait
as I shove back the soil
into the scar of the hole that moss will cover

and someone might watch
our little cortege
head back to the house your mother dressed

and warmed all those years
now she's a little mixed
with its beloved soil and each step confirms

possession is temporary
even a place of rest
you lean against the car as if out of breath

Always you

We half circle the lake this evening
exactly as we planned to do

but no one has given much thought
to this moment—divided by doubt

whether it's better to push ahead
or better turn back the way we came

the kind of question we always find
hard to fathom on balance we go on

yet talking now of the time you saw
how lit up the city's streets become

on nights like this under such low cloud
what to make of this austere moral

III
Boy-racer

Listening to Tippett twice

A Child of Our Time (1944)

At South Kensington now
I'm early to the table
wait patiently with a beer
then rise with a kiss to greet her

and my day's been real
in the absence of dreams
so ordinary real
to include the buying of bread

making a few calls
coffee and the newspapers'
rancour and grief
and time always fixing times

now the wash of notes
rises tentatively
from the well of the hall
though it's hard to give them

the attention they need
with these nervous coughs
percussive gunshots
yet as muted trumpets

lift the choir to its feet
I've gone a thousand miles
I run twenty years
into the sunlight

of a baked-brown hillside
near Assisi I remember
as a sloping orchard
near the end of summer

at the mouth of a tent
I gaze at sweltering heat
alone yet thinking of her
beyond the Alps

over the grey Channel
my earphones growling
with these same notes
I've no money for my bread

I've no gift for my love
the poor boy's plight
on the spooling tape
running steadily down

like a little clock of longing
though within a week
I'll have re-crossed Europe
falling into her arms

settling on the path
to where this tenor's lament
asks the same redemption
of two hundred voices

replying as one
these voices concluding
at last with silence
that pause of reluctance

as we pick up the threads
of the evening we realise
what our hands are for
this deferring of words

unless used in a way
to repeat the gift
of the dreamwork
of the singers against

the dreamwork of the past
to fling it forward
against rancour and grief
against the coming need

Summerhouse

The stream's bed is white and dry with dust
a billion leaves take the sunlight and shiver

with the vibration of insect life on all sides
the one ascending into the other's sphere

such warmth unfolds round each vital thing
with this electric life of desire you secure

drowned wings from the pool to dry in the sun
yet look again and the air has welcomed back

their gaudy fluttering and despite your gaze
they go stumbling to the lethal waters again

Four songs

Reveille

Flat shoes hush
to the emergency ward
since no good doctor
worth her salt

wears heels these days
daybreak or noon
the sun's feeble shafts
step into the room

Rolling news

We were right all along
society composed
not to think of itself
we saw it commit harm

no concern for another
the fuel's all gone
burned the best of ourselves
we were right all along

A town called Carresse

I have been living here
for so many years
just off the elegant
main squares

so long I've laboured
saved steadily
for this grander place
in the country

Lock down

At the cast-iron crash
of shutters closing
I learn life and death
with my neighbour

drill as per instruction
a black-gloved thumb
snug in the recess
of a mercenary gun

Philips *Electronic Engineer*

boys of today look to be engineers of tomorrow

The composite wooden board
carefully designed to stand on bakelite legs
to raise it one inch from the table
to let fingers under to feel out the future
by assembling components
threading them through pre-drilled holes
till rainbow-ringed resistors mated
with the gleam of spider-legged transistors
and little silver-blue tubs of capacitors
each according to the numbered charts
wired to the positioned weight
of blue and red Evereadies—
I'd labour at this through sweltering days
eager to clip the microphone
to the provided wire to thrust it
through the opened window above my bed
to adjust the angle in anticipation
of loose talk in the garden below
or better still from neighbours where they loafed
in the sun while I hunkered
in the shape of science at the speaker's mouth
all that summer of 1971
I scooped no more than the lisping
of white noise from the estate's patchwork
of lawns the dull surf of the A-road to town
and the *chup-chup* of sparrows
where they'd congregate in the gutter's shade
their unintelligible transmissions
as dusk fell as years later it falls
my ears no better tuned to scratching in the eaves
this vanishing business of crammed days
these records of winged numbers in decline

Boy-racer

It's *this* has been
snarling about our bed
shearing sleep
to fourths and sixteenths

until we crack
we climb in the car
head for the beach
he roars back to mock us

in a burst of cylinders
red—chrome—black—
bobbing back-wheel
bouncing dangerously

skids on to the road
from some blind track
this boy-racer bare-
headed breaking sixty

squirms in his seat
dodging flies and grit
grimacing back at us
as he whips left

right now he guns
through glittering traffic
his face all grin
above a dark brake light

left arm threading
a black helmet by his side
speed and dust please
his bald black bride

The boy from Wapakoneta

What he said was *man* instead of *a man*
so spawned these forty years of debate

since he was sure he said *a man* out loud
yet the recording has *man* and nothing more

which we took to imply the human race
losing sight of the contrast with mankind

who that day—his point—took a giant leap
while he trod dust under one small step

so did he merely fluff the greatest of lines
or did his Ohio accent blur what was said

or does his indefinite article hover there
launched forever and falling short

or did he subconsciously prefer
the phrase the lilt of that *step for man*

more like Auden who I read somewhere
would often destroy the sense of a line

he'd wrench denial into affirmation
to sweeten further his music for mankind

The girl who returned to Aix

Cezanne often painted Monte Sainte-Victoire, Aix-en-Provence

Even in the moment she tries to describe it
my eyes prefer a different mountain
one I watched snug and warm as Richard Dreyfus
was driven crazy by shapes in his head

in Spielberg's film of *Close Encounters*
though at this distance I still try to listen
to her conjuring the tip-toe child she was then
gazing at it through her bedroom window

in love with it she said—later to discover
his unfolding blue from blue as conjurors can
blues becoming greens by what sleight of hand

he could blend cone sphere and cylinder
to an alluring dance of blue *you don't look at*
she laughs now *so much as live through*

★

But the consolations of childhood and art
mean there's no better place for her to heal
suddenly adrift suddenly she's ill
in need of shelter from one-sided calls

I catch her talking to Montgomery Clift
to Monroe till horrified parents appear
and drive her home to where the artist daubed
his mountain and I lose my chance to tell

my story how once I gawped with pleasure
at that lovely ship rising like a crown
over the blacked-out shape of my mountain peak

and under Watford rain everything ran
in my eyes—I wept for that perfect thing
so perfectly pure where it hung in the air

In fact no more than a metre-wide model
a thing of smoke and mirrors gathering dust
in the director's garage—something to learn
how vision's a sampling of the ordinary

in extraordinary light but she could not
till she scared me with that alien glint in her eye
inventing tales like the day she declared
she had a plane to catch that afternoon

how a yellow cab would be waiting
it would sport this badge on this dented grille
set fair for the foothills of Santa Monica

the last in a line of extraordinary moves
for its special fare—for all I know she's still
smoothing her knees staring up through the air

Check-in

Heathrow—somewhere near

The spray-shape
of a yellow aerosol
on the riser
of the down escalator
disappears from view
every fifty-eight seconds
I've seen it slip
from each completed
minute by two seconds
with each rotation
a thing I can't ignore
watching it vanish
my bag beside me
as I settled at the outset
the red second hand
stroking seven
till the yellow smear
now dips from sight
as the hand touches three
so fully ten times
the escalator's run
its course as this
overweight man descends
wearing new trainers
his white toe tapping
three steps above
the formlessness
of my yellow scuff
my daub shaped a little
like a bear an orchid

a folded glove
all the while biting
the apple held firm
in his right hand
its skin the green
of the tee-shirt I'm sure
he bought yesterday
and by the time
he's made his way
from the metal staircase
my yellow swoosh
has dipped once more
sped off in pursuit
of the gleaming treads
or perhaps it flees
the bright yellow splash
goes tucking under with
something of a swimmer's
rolling turn but I guess
already these words
he brings walking
straight to me his mouth
shaping *let be*
he's close now serious
he whispers *let be*

Verso Girona

As noiseless bronzed miles
slide rapidly past
they stand in lay-bys
as if waiting in the wild
each dressed with care
in this Catholic country
though not discreetly
and this is not the city
passing one then another
you realise slowly
at the fifth or sixth time
your stare's returned
by full-on shaded eyes
locked to your passing
the steady rise and fall
of the powerful engine
in their strappy tops
one clamped to a mobile
they talk to each other—
there's community here
as you hurry through
gunning south across
poorly-marked borders
no real destination
you try staring them out
like a single shot
like a bare possibility
while another car at speed
moves in the opposite
direction with its driver
and her husband
each barely registering
with two young girls
noisy in the back seats
asking every scrap
of their attention
how you pull across
how willingly declines
the smoked silent glass

Things difficult to love

In the catalogue of things difficult to love
you stand high
the moment I set eyes on you
crawling upside down
on the painted window frame
though I don't think you dangerous at first
just unpleasantly alien
with those eight ginger-tufted legs
clinging firm with eight black-period feet
splayed from a body

which is no more than a loosened knot
of gingery string equipped
with half-transparent mouth-parts
and how many eyes you have trained on me
on my daughter about whom you explore
after lights out in pursuit
of pheromone trails of possible mate
the scent of possible prey
like a drone examining
the quadrants of the barren room
you end up hanging head down
on her headboard close beside her hand

and it may be you pursue nothing more
than what you must
it may be we might be able to learn
from such a focus an enviable form
of self-realisation but see
how it involves this silent up-picking
of eight black-pointed feet
this crawling into my daughter's sleeping palm
till she senses each black daub
her hand closing and there
you writhe and bite her you bite her there
as she starts in the middle of the night
to find she's under attack

in the supposed animal safety of her bed
and my love of her
means my hand twitches with hers
my belly lurches with her fear of what unfolds

in the night as her forearm balloons
with her body's fighting back
and you have slipped away
yet with the dawn
I have grown more and more convinced
in the catalogue of things
difficult to love you stand high
and you will not be alone
I'm awake I'm ready I come to hunt you down

Street View

*http://maps.google.co.uk/maps?hl=en&q=street+view+brent+street
&bav=on.2,or.r_gc.r_pw.r_qf.&bpcl=37189454&biw=996&bih=9
21&um=1&ie=UTF-8&sa=N&tab=wl*

Just a few clicks and there I am
real and distant as I was on Brent Street
dawdling along
swinging my left arm

a few papers folded under the other
or perhaps it's a book
that a few minutes later I'll be reading
over coffee in a café out of sight

yet in this first this remotest shot
I'm still unaware
that I've been taken
though in this second a few metres on

a few moments closer to the present
where I sit at this untidy desk
troubling these keys to describe
the triumvirate

of self and other and time
what is clear is that I'm staring
that I've spotted the car's roof-top stem
so strangely equipped

with its fish-eye lens...
then in this third I'm stopped at the kerb
I let it swerve past at the corner
and though in each image

I am pixilated for my privacy's sake
there's something evident
in the way I stand suggests I've guessed
and my guessing's fixed

then posted how many months later
for the world to see
if you trouble to check the address—
I mean the web URL

not the OS coordinates—there's
no comparison between these screen shots
and the thrill I find
in maps or the topographical charms

and chants of the weather forecast
how I love to sniff a breeze
blustering in my mind off the Wash
or trudge blindly through drills

of dreamt-up Pennine rain
or relish the cold brief grit of licking flakes
from freezing gloves
all the while thinking myself across Shap—

it seems civilisation advances
at a slant until we think
our status raised with every outed image
till it feels important

not to have missed the breakfast news
with its rainy gantry shots
from cameras swung on servos
to update us about where the traffic's bad

where winking queues clog the roads
I'm soon to drive on my way to work
yet I have to confess
watching the silent swerve and criss-cross

of red lights as cars and lorries
shuffle like cards round Henley's Corner
or the sight of traffic
skirting cones at roadworks

or burst mains in Acton or Bayswater
gives me a peculiar thrill
in which I imagine one foggy morning
when I glimpse myself

driving where I've yet to be
and that's like staring at this desktop screen
to find myself
in the exact place I left months ago

and easy to compare this
to what seems the iconic shot of our age
when an attentive deliberate crowd
is absorbed

in a match or parade or demonstration
then someone's alert
in a quite different way
and she grins and the guy beside her waves

an inflatable hammer or one gloved hand
as she points off to one side
trying tentatively to assess
the position the exact angle of the lens

till they twist left then further left again
till satisfied they're gazing
full face from the screen we cannot see
beyond the screen we can

and their image shows there sharp as glass
dull as verse but admired
since it's ourselves we like to cheer
for nothing or no more than just being here

Acknowledgements

Some of these poems or earlier versions of them have appeared in: *Agenda, Ambit, antiphon* (http://www.antiphon.org.uk/), *Black Box Manifold, The Dark Horse, Eyewear* (http://www.eyewearpublishing.com/poems/), *The Glasgow Review of Books, Loch Raven Review* (USA), *London Grip, The London Magazine, Magma, New Walk, Poetry London, Poetry Wales, The Missing Slate* (http://themissingslate.com/), *The Rialto, Shearsman, South, Stand, The Stare's Nest* (https://thestaresnest.com/).

'La Gioconda gone' appeared in Post Hoc (Bank Street Arts, Sheffield, 2011/Sheffield Poetry Festival, 2011). 'The little dances' appeared in the Wordaid/ShelterBox anthology, *Not Only the Dark* (eds. Jo Field, Nicky Gould, 2011). 'Summerhouse' was commissioned for the 2012 Magma Magazine Poetry Competition and appeared in the anthology *Poets in Person*, edited by Aprilia Zank (Indigo Dreams Publishing, 2014). 'As we live' appeared in the Cheltenham Poetry Festival's anthology *Dear World* (Frosted Fire Press, 2015). 'Listening to Tippett twice' appeared in *Accompanied Voices: Poets on Composers*, ed. John Greening (Boydell Press, 2015). 'Mitigation' appeared in *Wheel of the Stars: 50th Anniversary Anthology of Ver Poets* (Ver Poets, 2016).

'Your dark-haired daughter' was short-listed in the 2010 Keats-Shelley Memorial Poetry Prize and later appeared (with 'House sold') in *The Book of Love and Loss*, eds. R.V. Bailey and June Hall (Belgrave Press, Bath, 2014).

'Script' (as 'Cars at the roadside') was commended in the 2011 Barnet Open Poetry Competition. 'R-O-M-J-X' was commended in the 2012 Hippocrates Poetry Competition. 'The lovely disciplines' was a prize winner in the 2013 Kent and Sussex Poetry Competition. 'In "Any Amount of Books"' was highly commended in the 2014 Segora International Poetry Competition. 'The toll cottage' was commended in the Cafe Writers' Poetry Competition 2014. 'These things I remember' was commended in the 2015 Segora International Poetry Competition and draws on material from *The Letters of Edward Thomas to Jesse Berridge* (Enitharmon Press, 1983).